Broken I

words of love and pro

DM McGill

www.danmcgill.com

2014

First published in 2014
by Biff Bang Books

for you....and you.....and you

Contents

Grand Hotel

The way she shakes so,
is indicative of her age.
But in the morning she is still.
Then her body unwinds,
and springs into action.

She wakes before me,
then wakes me with her soft gurgling.
And the force of water against stainless steel.
And the pad of her feet past my bedroom door.

I think of the contrivance Gilbert O'Sullivan made,
when he sang a love song –
only to reveal its subject was a child.

I choose no sucker punch.
The gurgling is the sound her throat makes,
when she wakes.
And the pad

Valentines Day, 2014

Cold Camden Town,
basement kitchen.
Breath freezing.
Steam rising,
from a coffee cup.

I climb the stairs
of my broken-down house.
Hair dishevelled.
Face unshaven.
Legs stiff and unyielding.

The heater has taken
that chill from my room.
Plastic window covering,
crinkles.
Cars move outside.

I place a twelve inch
on the turntable.
Forget Me Nots,
by Patrice Rushen.
It's for you.

The Pieces he will never play

I imagine him standing in the Turbine Hall
playing an asbestos Violin.
Connected to the loudest of sound-systems.

He's dressed in a boiler suit,
that suits the buildings former use.
And a Station Master's cap.

And despite the amplification,
not a single sound issues –
from his violin.

Instead there's a low hum,
reminiscent of something moving
at incredible speed.

Then silence.
Then pain.
Then nothing.

I imagine he wants to explain
why this cavernous space.
Smells of smoke and burning flesh.

Why a carelessly discarded cigarette,
and a journey from Highbury to Kings Cross.
Ended at Sodom and Gomorrah.

And I think about the pieces,
he will never play.
While cradling his silent violin.

On hearing Lord Dyson's ruling that appeals against the Bedroom Tax were "manifestly without reasonable foundation."

When is a society, a Civil Society?

When rulers don't wage war on the people they are supposed to be ruling?

When the needs of those deemed most venerable, are considered?

When efforts are made to establish peaceful coexistence, are not overturned?

When reality rather than ideology is used to determine policy?

When the Courts of Appeal uphold the law, not bad government?

When despair does not colour every day?

Memory Burning

The brother he liked Graceland,
played it every day as I recall.
It never surprised me
that he'd taken so long to discover.
The memory forms a window,
that opens up into a courtyard.

Night falls and the lights are turned out.
Downstairs a kettle boils,
and she sits smoking at the table.
Her face is creased with the night.

Laminate
Chip-board veneer.
Hound-dog collection.
A small christening spoon of tarnished silver.

Memory burning away in the cigarette light.
Small flecks of ash falling onto trouser legs.
A forgotten conversation round the kitchen table.
Maybe I deliberately choose to forget.

Her head was tiny,
so small with fine wisps of hair.
Impossibly narrow shoulders.
A small hipless body,
with a smell so rare
It's hard to forget.

I return to the courtyard,
full of bikes and broken down contraptions.
A washing line and a savaged garden.
Dog excrement.
And the rotting stump of a tree.

On the step sits a man smoking.
The vapour rises to the heavens,
trailing three stories high.
Touching god in the process.
Smoke is the theme of this place.
Smoke and the fact things are broken and never repaired,
Left out in the open and rained on.

On Saturdays they have a market,
selling cauliflowers and CDs.
The Graceland LP.
And flamenco dresses fit for children.
In the courtyard I hear the sound of castanets clicking.

After Joy Division

Radio transmission
seeks out new listeners,
as night tightens it's noose.

A sine wave.
A square wave.
A synaptic dance.

The radio plays
to the static man.
One of his old tunes.

His child wakes with a cry.
His wife waves for help.
His radio plays on and on.

Django

Django played in the tunnels beneath Bank Station.
He fashioned a twisted scale,
that drifted on the air.
And he made me think of Morocco,
and the sweet fragrant smell of Marrakech.

Django: all awkward and angular,
with a mop of thick blond hair.
Had large bony fingers,
that made me think of Christ's,
bending round the cross.

Django hummed as he played.
More moan than tune.
It sounded raw and real, and how he could feel the music.
And he made me think of the Mississippi delta,
and the wide expanse of river rolling along.

Django spoke silently to me,
 and I to him.
We acknowledged each other,
as familiar strangers do.
With a nod of our heads.

One Christmas.
He wore a velvet hat Trimmed with ermine fur,
and an Arabian cloak to keep out the cold.
And I though of Gold, Incense, Frankincense and myrrh.
And things like joy and goodwill to all like Django.

[15]

Django was the name,
sent telepathically to me.
And I thought of Django Reinhart,
and his paralyzed fingers,
and of those who are not as fortunate as he.

Django busked during the winter of 1984,
while miners struck and the GLC crumbled.
And the memory of him, brings into focus,
this current hard winter,
and how warm it is underground.

NiteWalk Thieves

NiteWalk thieves,
and the roll of a cummerbund.
The dark purple,
softly quilted,
holds everything together.

And yet.
I do recall,
the photographs on her wall.
And the NiteWalk thieves,
making exits, unseen.

The Last Imbiber

On the day Dennis Hopper died,
I drink two beers with my meal.
And purchase another three for later.

I eat a Betty Rocker white chocolate cookie,
laced with marijuana.
Then quaff three beers,
one-by-one.

I attempt to operate a Blue Ray DVD player,
and fail.
But drink two glasses of Spanish Cava,
successfully.

A few thousand miles away,
Dennis Hopper lies cold –
alive no more.
And I raise my final glass.
To the last of the great imbibers I say.

Beatsox

They live in the corner,
where your hand can't reach.
Behind the washing machine.
Inside old suit cases,
stuffed away and forgotten.
They disappear down the side of your bed;
a hairs-breath away from your slumbering head.
You may hear them scuttle,
as your finger touches the light switch:
a muffled, soft cotton-wool burr.
And when the night comes,
they come out.
They roll and roll,
until the embers of dawn begin to glow.
Then scuttle away in light flight.
They are the beat-up old sock you thought was lost,
the ones that never return from a wash.

C

Ah ha.
Ha.
Look its you,
sitting there.
You great fucking thing.

What are you doing there?
Relaxing,
are you ?
Enjoying this.
are you?

The Therapist

You call yourself a therapist.
Yet you watch me,
with a Policeman's eye.

You take down notes,
and ask questions.
But hear nothing that I say.

How can you
describe yourself as a therapist.
When you're no more than a form-filler.

Where's the occupation
in your occupation.
I want to scream.

But I keep quiet
while you tick one box
after another.

And at the end,
you say:
What type of cancer was it.

You call yourself a therapist.
Yet you can't even read,
my consultant's letter.

And where's the occupation
in your occupation.
When all you are is a fucking apparatchik.

[21]

Not There

Hi Missy E, you weren't there.
So I had no problem
avoiding you're 1000 yard stare.
Lord Plumb-in-his-mouth
read all the Jamaican stuff.
And we all missed you madly.
I think even she (who must be obeyed)
missed you for a second.
Then Maria arrived out of a cake,
all dressed up like Sally Bowles.
She read a little from "I know how the cage bird
sings"
Even tried on your accent, ha.
But it came out all posh.
Not a bit like Maya Angelou,
or you.

Ebay item number: 2964019683

The child's chair
sits in her room,
stuffing knocked-out.

A miniature adult,
upholstered in maroon.
Hidden away.

Once owned by us three,
it was passed-on,
to her and me.

So it stays with us two,
always there.
Her maroon little chair.

Karen Sings

Karen leans her fleshy arms against mine.
She has nut brown hair,
and a plain blue dress.
And is just as she was -
when we all had new skin on our faces.

And here I am,
nuzzling – smelling – experiencing it all.
Burrowing my tiny head into her.

Karen sings in a soft girl's voice,
loud above the roar and rattle of others.

And there I was,
watching her perform.
Impervious to everything outside ourselves.

Karen presses her thick lips against mine.
She sucks the air from me,
so all I have is her taste and delicious asphyxiation.

And here I am again,
with my top lip bleeding,
struggling to breathe.

Karen sings to a boy with brilliant blond hair.
Then turns to me and puckers.

Karen sings to everyone,
But she kisses only me.

On the death of Nick Potter

On the death of Nick Potter,
bassist with Van der Graaf.
I first play a song.
Then read his obituary.
So slight, but with an essence of him.

Then I turn to wikipedia.
And read about the disease,
that ate away his brain.
Leaving him dead from pneumonia,
aged 61.

And I want to leave it this way, but I can't.
So I press play again.
And listen to Darkness (11/11),
recorded in Germany,
back when he was nineteen.

And the music spurs me on.
I need to check his birth-date on wikipedia,
so I go back and read some more.
And at the very end,
I find a scenario familiar to me.

Admitted in winter to a ward at UCH.
He, unlike me, never bids farewell to the nurses.
Or worries about the brand of chocolates to buy.
Instead there begins a new journey,
for the man who loved to travel.

Cinderella in repose

I'm slumped against the tube wall,
at 12 midnight.
Carriages turn into pumpkins,
and mice scurry about.
A man dressed in a tutu,
waves a silver magic wand.

Princesses go home with princes,
And the rest:

They fill the platforms.
They blink in the brightest artificial daylight.
They talk and jabber.
Or stand silently, or sway silently, or sing
incoherently.

At 12'O one,
the last High Barnet train is gone.
The one I should be on.
Instead I lean against a fire-hose,
and watch Cinderella, in repose.

The storms of England

The storms of England
make the news.
A national meltdown.
A railway line gone.

The storms of England
can't be quelled.
With water cannon.
Or surveillance.

The storms of England
refused to be buried.
With razzmatazz.
Instead they pass verdict:

On those guilty of inhumanity
and crimes against the poor.
Those doers of death,
and venal incompetence.

The storms of England
will wash away we hope.
Those who use patriotism,
as a refuge from the torrent.

I can hear it coming

At night, as I lie awake in bed,
I listen to the sound of the railway.
Rolling thunder and screeching metal wheels.
It reminds me of a time before the Great Recession;
when I had to imagine how poverty and pain felt.

Morning V3

Was a cold cold morning,   this morning,
on my way down to the tube.
A man with a suitcase and crocodile shoes,
shone through the still-night frost.
I looked closer at his shoes,
and saw the girl with jaguar hair.
Reclining, with a drink, on her sofa.
He took out a guitar from his suitcase,
and played me: Wild horses couldn't drag me
away.
I smiled sadly and made my way,
away from the girl with the jaguar hair.
But maybe,
one day?

How We Go

The rhythm is what matters.
Because we are creatures of
habit.

First we follow the flow
of life.
The behaviour of nature.

Then we watch the movement
of stars.
As they turn in the sky.

Finally we look inwards.
And observe our internal
beat.

Its process becomes apparent
Its motion,
is not at all unique.

[30]

Dead Rock corner

He died on the crapper
Elvis did.
Reading a paper
as you do.

Carl Perkins
fell dead drunk down the stairs
and lay there for a couple of weeks,
until his body oozed out.

Then there was Bill Haley and his comet.
Wow was his wife surprised,
when he chose to spontaneously combust.
Into a pile of dust and a pair of blue suede shoes.

They once belonged to Eddie Cochran
who's last hit was the tree.
Which is a joke stolen from Marc Bolan.
late of Barnes and Beltane way.

Slipping on a Yen

The rapid snatch of a glass spittoon.
The green grind manacle.
The grey and white grey matter.
Boxers reclining against ropes.

Sliver stream, slipstream.
Delivery light and the night.
Fixing its swollen eye on the things that twist and fall.
I shake into the distance, swaying on the margins.

Crystal clear HD.
Extinct species with finite resources.
Stoat filled lizard brain.
Macaw claw, four to the floor.

Snake brain, beard.
Bees and these and pollination.
Pesticides killing.
Wildflowers collapse, diets crash.

Charismatic megaphore slipping on a yen.
Bad teeth, giant and beautiful.
Clapping eye.
Shooting them in the wild.

Up-close - orangutans and gorillas.
Conservation – twenty million.
Rent a million sell a thousand
Purple tights and crossed over legs.

You believe them,
That's what you do.
When you know it's all an act.
The broken muscular sentence, hanging on its side.

Salutation Station

To all the girls on the underground,
I've never married.
I salute you.

To the fluffers,
cleaning at night.
I salute you.

To the Ticket Master,
writing poetry at Tufnell Park.
I salute you.

To the men and women,
helping pushchairs take the stairs.
I salute you.

To the drivers and announcers,
the back-roomers and maintenance crews.
I salute you.

To that spare seat in a crowded carriage,
and the lady who smells of Channel Number 5.
I salute you.

To the driver who emptied his train at Farringdon,
on the seventh of July two thousand and five.
I salute you.

To the Irish, Asian,
and Windrush navigators.
I salute you.

To the train that takes me to Warren Street,
for treatment at UCH.
I salute you.

To the journey planner,
and underground maps.
I salute you.

To the Chinese restaurant and pizza joints,
and to all the other abandoned stations.
I salute you.

And to the hundred million passengers,
who travel underground everyday.
I salute you !

6106585R00021

Printed in Great Britain
by Amazon.co.uk, Ltd.,
Marston Gate.